MW01492841

# SUBWAY SYSTEM

## BY CECILIA PINTO MCCARTHY

**CONTENT CONSULTANT**
Gene Sansone
Adjunct Professor of Civil and Urban Engineering
NYU Tandon School of Engineering

**Core Library**

Cover image: A New York City subway train pulls into a station.

An Imprint of Abdo Publishing
abdopublishing.com

abdopublishing.com

Published by Abdo Publishing, a division of ABDO, PO Box 398166,
Minneapolis, Minnesota 55439. Copyright © 2018 by Abdo Consulting
Group, Inc. International copyrights reserved in all countries. No part of this
book may be reproduced in any form without written permission from the
publisher. Core Library™ is a trademark and logo of Abdo Publishing.

Printed in the United States of America, North Mankato, Minnesota
042017
072018

THIS BOOK CONTAINS
RECYCLED MATERIALS

Distributed in paperback by North Star Editions, Inc.

Cover Photo: Shutterstock Images
Interior Photos: Shutterstock Images, 1; Waring Abbott/Michael Ochs Archives/Getty Images,
4–5, 43; John Kirk/iStockphoto, 8–9, 45; Kean Collection/Archive Photos/Getty Images, 12–13;
Bettmann/Getty Images, 14, 32; Mark Lennihan/AP Images, 17; Science & Society Picture Library/
SSPL/Getty Images, 20; David Pollack/Corbis Historical/Getty Images, 22–23; Red Line Editorial, 24;
iStockphoto, 26; Keystone/Hulton Archive/Getty Images, 29; Melanie Stetson Freeman/The Christian
Science Monitor/Getty Images, 34–35; Howard Earl Simmons/NY Daily News Archive/Getty Images,
37; Richard B. Levine/Newscom, 38–39

Editor: Heidi Schoof
Imprint Designer: Maggie Villaume
Series Design Direction: Laura Polzin

Publisher's Cataloging-in-Publication Data

Names: McCarthy, Cecilia Pinto, author.
Title: Engineering the NYC Subway System / by Cecilia Pinto McCarthy.
Description: Minneapolis, MN : Abdo Publishing, 2018. | Series: Building by
  design | Includes bibliographical references and index.
Identifiers: LCCN 2017930243 | ISBN 9781532111686 (lib. bdg.) |
  ISBN 9781641852562 (pbk) | ISBN 9781680789539 (ebook)
Subjects:  LCSH: Structural engineering--Miscellanea--Juvenile literature. |
  Subways (New York (N.Y.)--Design and  construction--Juvenile literature. |
  Civil engineering--Juvenile literature. | Buildings, structures, etc.--Juvenile
  literature. | Buildings--Miscellanea--Juvenile literature.
Classification: DDC 624--dc23
  LC record available at http://lccn.loc.gov/2017930243

# CONTENTS

# AN AMAZING SYSTEM

**S**creech! Metal scrapes against metal as the subway train grinds into the Times Square–42nd Street station. The sound drowns out the voice of a guitar-strumming musician. A businessman drops the musician a few coins. Nearby, a tourist pulls out a smartphone. She snaps a picture of the mural overhead. The vivid mural looks like a strip from a comic book. People hustle by the tourist. They hope to catch the next train. It's Friday night rush hour in New York City.

Crowds of people stand at the station. A voice over the loudspeaker warns, "Please

Each day, millions of people move through New York City's subway system.

## PERSPECTIVES
### A LONG WAIT

The New York City subway system has long had difficulties keeping up with increasing ridership. The East Side in particular has been plagued by overcrowding and delays. In 1920 officials made a plan to ease the problem. They would build a Second Avenue subway line. But the project was postponed several times. Many New Yorkers were skeptical it would ever be built. The first phase of the project finally opened for service on January 1, 2017. It is New York City's biggest subway expansion in 50 years. When all phases are complete, the Second Avenue line will extend service along Manhattan's East Side by 8.5 miles (13.7 km).

stand away from the platform edge." The train doors open wide. A river of travelers flows onto the platform. Waiting passengers nudge their way into the train. When each subway car is packed, the doors shut. The train clacks off to the next station.

The Times Square–42nd Street station lies at the heart of midtown Manhattan. It is New York City's busiest subway station. Each year more than 66 million passengers get on and off at Times Square. The New York City subway system has a total of 472 stations. This is the most of any subway system in the world.

## THE SUBWAY NEVER SLEEPS

New York City cannot function without its subway system. Workers, shoppers, and sightseers rely on it 24 hours a day. In 2015 more than 1.7 billion passengers rode its 661 miles (1,063 km) of rails. More than half of the system lies underground.

Interest in building subways began in the mid-1800s. Many major cities worldwide were overcrowded. Traffic jams were common. City leaders decided to build underground transportation tunnels. Traveling underground would relieve crowding on busy streets. In 1863 the world's first subway system opened in London, England. New York City was also suffering from jam-packed streets. But its first subway would not open until October 27, 1904.

Some portions of the subway system include above-ground sections of track.

Most people who ride the subway probably do not give much thought to how it was built. The creation of the New York City subway system was a long and complex feat of engineering. Civil engineer William Barclay Parsons took on the challenge. As chief engineer, Parsons planned and oversaw every phase of construction. Parsons's deputy chief engineer was George S. Rice. Rice had previous experience with

building subways. He had supervised the construction of the subway system in Boston, Massachusetts.

Parsons and his team were highly skilled engineers. They set out to solve New York City's transportation problems. The engineers calculated the pressure that soil, rock, and water would exert on subway tunnels. They considered the weight of streets and vehicles, as well as the weight of trains and passengers.

# CIVIL ENGINEERING

Civil engineering deals with the design and construction of structures people use every day. It is one of the oldest types of engineering. Civil engineers design and build bridges, buildings, dams, subways, and highways. Many engineers specialize in particular industries. Coastal engineers understand how waves and storms affect structures. Transportation engineers focus on making travel safe and efficient. Environmental engineers work to keep air and water clean.

The strongest building materials would be used to support the subway. Electrical experts were in charge of powering subway trains and stations. Parsons and his team of engineers applied math and science skills to understand, plan, and successfully execute this colossal construction project.

# STRAIGHT TO THE
# SOURCE

William Barclay Parsons knew that building New York City's first subway line was just the beginning of a long-lasting engineering project. In May 1900, Parsons wrote that there would always be a need for more and better subway lines:

> *For years there has been a cry for more transportation . . . to give relief to the crowds. . . . This relief the proposed underground railroad will give but temporarily. . . . The instant that this line is finished, there will arise a demand for other lines, and so on until the northward growth of the city reaches . . . beyond the Harlem River. . . . The present plan for the subway . . . is not a finality in any sense. Betterments, additions, extensions, and even parallel lines will be added in the future, as the continuing, insatiable demand for more facilities requires.*

Source: William Barclay Parsons. "Rapid Transit in New York." *Scribner's Magazine.* Google Books, May 1900. Web. Accessed February 13, 2017.

## What's the Big Idea?
Read this passage carefully. What is Parsons saying about what will happen once the first subway line is finished? What does he predict will happen in the future? Why?

# PREPARING TO BUILD

I n the 1800s, the Industrial Revolution brought people to New York City. Machines and factories changed daily life. More workers moved into cities. By 1880 New York City was home to more than 1.2 million people. It was the largest city in the United States. People traveled on foot, by horse-drawn vehicle, or on elevated trains. Streets were a mess of people, horses, and manure. City filth made people ill.

In March 1888, a devastating blizzard struck New York City. It covered the city in more than 21 inches (53 cm) of snow. Massive snow piles and downed electrical

The Industrial Revolution led to new transportation demands in New York City.

The brutal blizzard of 1888 made underground trains look like an attractive option.

wires paralyzed the city. People were trapped indoors for days.

New York City's transportation system needed to change. The only solution was to go underground. The first route would be 9.1 miles (14.6 km) long. It would extend from City Hall to 145th Street in Harlem. A few years later, it would be lengthened to 21 miles (34 km).

## PARSONS'S PLANS

Such a huge project required a careful plan. Before excavation could begin, Parsons had to understand the geology of Manhattan. What was underground?

Parsons's crew conducted a geological survey. They studied

## BEACH'S PNEUMATIC SUBWAY

New York inventor Alfred Ely Beach made the first attempt to build a subway under New York City. In 1870 Beach opened a trial one-track subway. The brick-lined tunnel was short, just 312 feet (95 m). The single, cylinder-shaped car was powered by pneumatic power. A huge blower forced air into the tunnel, shooting the train car forward. When the blower was reversed, the car would be sucked back to the other end of the track. Beach was never able to gain enough support to expand his railway. He eventually went bankrupt and closed his tunnel.

Manhattan's landforms. The land was not flat. It had hills and valleys. Surveyors took measurements. Parsons examined test samples dug from the earth. The samples provided information about the soil, rock, and water underground. These conditions would influence the subway's route and depth.

Manhattan's geology posed challenges. It varied a great deal. Below the surface lay solid rock called bedrock. It was schist. This is a hard rock created under heat and pressure. In several areas, the schist was layered. The layers could easily shift. Tunneling through schist would be difficult and dangerous.

Also, the location of schist differed from place to place. In mid- and lower Manhattan, schist was just 18 feet (5.5 m) below the surface. In other areas, schist was 260 feet (79 m) underground. The survey also showed areas of loose, wet soil. These areas would not be stable enough for digging.

Major construction projects in Manhattan often involve digging down to the island's bedrock.

## FINDING SOLUTIONS

Parsons devised a solution. He drew up plans for a subway route close to the surface. A shallow subway had many advantages. Tunneling through schist could be avoided in some areas. Subway stations would not need expensive elevators. Instead, passengers could enter and exit quickly using staircases. Being near the surface meant fresh air and natural light could enter the stations more easily.

Still, engineers had other issues to solve before digging could begin. They designed viaducts to carry trains over Manhattan's valleys. Workers moved telegraph and electrical lines. They rerouted water, sewer, gas, and steam pipes. Buildings near construction zones needed extra support. Heavy timbers and steel beams were set up to hold foundations in place.

## CLEAN POWER

Parsons chose electricity as the subway's energy source. He had studied rail systems in Europe. Trains that burned coal created soot and pollution. However, Britain's City and South London railway used electricity. Parsons was impressed by the cleanliness, convenience, and low cost of electrical energy. Electrical experts installed the subway's electrical power. Electricity would do more than move trains. It would also light the stations and power equipment.

## A FOUR-TRACK SYSTEM

Parsons' subway design was like no other. He devised a four-track system. Trains would travel on two tracks going in each direction. The outer tracks provided local service. These trains would stop at every station.

The center tracks carried express trains. These traveled farther and faster, with fewer stops.

When it opened, the New York City subway system would be a true wonder. It became the model for future subway systems. It would work efficiently because of the design of its tracks and cars, stations, entrances, and power supply.

## EXPLORE ONLINE

Chapter Two discusses why New York City needed a subway system. The website below talks about how technology helped solve New York's transportation issue. What information does the website give about transportation in New York City during the 1800s? How is the information the same as the information in Chapter Two? What new information did you learn from the website?

## BUILDING THE BIG APPLE: SUBWAYS
abdocorelibrary.com/engineering-the-nyc-subway-system

Parsons was impressed by the electric trains in London, England.

# CHAPTER
# THREE

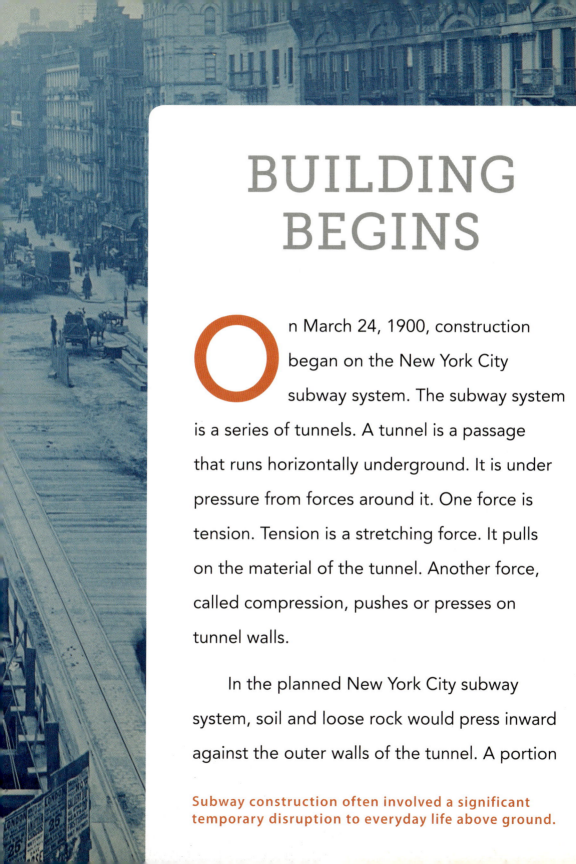

# BUILDING BEGINS

**O**n March 24, 1900, construction began on the New York City subway system. The subway system is a series of tunnels. A tunnel is a passage that runs horizontally underground. It is under pressure from forces around it. One force is tension. Tension is a stretching force. It pulls on the material of the tunnel. Another force, called compression, pushes or presses on tunnel walls.

In the planned New York City subway system, soil and loose rock would press inward against the outer walls of the tunnel. A portion

# FORCES ON A TUNNEL

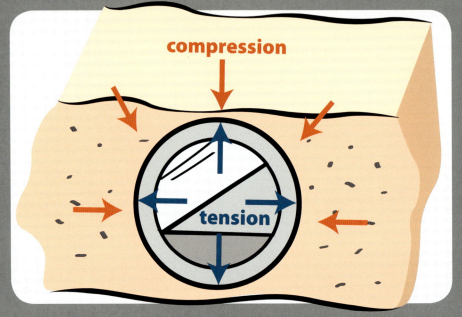

This diagram shows forces that act on an underground tunnel. Engineers building the New York City subway had to balance these forces. What force pushes in on the sides of the tunnel? What would happen if there were not enough tension pushing back on the tunnel walls?

of the subway would have to travel under the East River. There the tunnel would be compressed by both soil and water.

Forces called loads also act on subway tunnels. Loads may be dead or live. Dead loads are stationary. They always act on a structure. The weight of the tunnel itself is a type of dead load. Live loads are moving loads. They act on a structure temporarily. People and traffic moving over a tunnel are live loads.

Tunneling is a dangerous job. Too much compression can cause tunnels to buckle and collapse. Engineers design strong tunnels by balancing the forces that act on them. A tunnel must be able to resist the forces exerted on it.

The shape of a tunnel gives it support. Parsons and his engineers designed tunnels with arch-shaped roofs, or crowns. This shape would spread out the weight pushing down on the tunnel. Materials played a part in keeping the tunnels strong. The tunnels would be lined with concrete to keep water out and prevent them from collapsing.

## CUT-AND-COVER EXCAVATION

The method for building a subway near the road surface was cut-and-cover excavation. Thousands of laborers used hand tools to break up Manhattan's streets. First they dug trenches. Then they covered the openings

# CUT-AND-COVER EXCAVATION

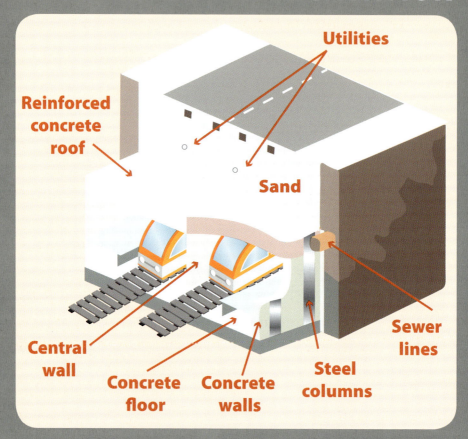

**Utilities**

**Reinforced concrete roof**

**Sand**

**Central wall**

**Concrete floor**

**Concrete walls**

**Steel columns**

**Sewer lines**

This diagram shows cut-and-cover excavation both above and below ground. How does seeing the drawing help you better understand what you learned from the text? What are some of the benefits of using this method? Can you think of any disadvantages to this type of excavation?

with large beams. On especially busy streets, workers put up temporary wooden roadways to carry traffic. City life continued aboveground while construction took place underground.

After clearing the rubble, or spoils, workers spread a four-inch (10-cm) concrete foundation. The concrete provided sturdy support for the track. A layer of thick felt soaked with hot asphalt was laid down. It sealed the concrete from moisture.

Terra cotta walls were installed next. Electrical cables were threaded through hollow tubes in the walls to provide power for the subway. To withstand load forces, the tunnel framework was constructed out of strong steel. Between the roof beams, concrete arches

## CONCRETE AND STEEL: A DYNAMIC DUO

Concrete is made of cement, water, sand, and gravel. The cement and water mix to form a tight bond with the sand and gravel. The mixture hardens into concrete. Concrete is ideal for construction. It is cheap and extremely strong. It can resist the force of weight pressing down on it. But concrete cracks easily when bent or stretched. This problem is solved by combining concrete with steel bars to make reinforced concrete. Reinforced concrete can withstand the pressures of bending and stretching.

strengthened the subway roof. Some concrete was reinforced with steel rods.

Finally, the steel train tracks were placed and secured with spikes. Special tracks made of steel mixed with a metal called manganese were used along curves. These tracks were strong enough to withstand the scraping of wheels against rails on corners. For added protection, guard rails were installed at corners. A cement wall was built between sets of tracks. It would act as a barrier in case of a crash.

## THE TUNNELING METHOD

Cut-and-cover excavation was not always practical. Along the route, workers sometimes had to make adjustments. Some areas were too soft or wet to hold a trench. In mid- and lower Manhattan, schist bedrock blocked the way. In these cases, the tunneling method was used.

A thick steel cylinder called a shield was lowered piece by piece into the ground. The pieces were

Tunneling under New York City was dark, difficult work.

assembled into a sharp-edged tube. At the front end, the shield protected workers from falling rocks and loose soil. They used pneumatic drills and dynamite to clear the way. Compressed air pushed the sharp-edged shield forward. Behind the shield, workers put sections of the tunnel into place.

## SANDHOGS WORKED UNDER PRESSURE

The men who worked in underground shields were known as sandhogs. They faced danger every day for very little pay. Sometimes water would seep into the tunnel. To stop the flow, compressed air would be pumped in. The pressure would be much higher than normal air pressure. To protect themselves, sandhogs rested in underground airlocks. Inside the lock, the pressure was gradually lowered or raised. This gave their bodies time to adjust. If the pressure changed too quickly, they would get air bubbles in their blood. This caused a painful condition called the bends. Sandhogs with the bends suffered joint pain, paralysis, and sometimes death.

At Lenox Avenue, Parsons and his engineers faced a new problem. How could they continue the subway across the Harlem River? This challenge demanded a different tunneling technique. First, a 50-foot (15-m) trench was dredged 39 feet (12 m) below the water. Premade tunnel sections were carried out on the river on barges. Then they were sunk into the trench. After the water was pumped out of the tunnel, it was lined with concrete. The ends were connected to the subway tunnels on either side of the river.

## POWERING THE SUBWAY

While Parsons concentrated on construction, electrical experts worked on powering the system. A power plant was built just for the subway. It was built along the Hudson River and used the river's water in its boilers. The boilers, fueled by burning coal, produced steam. The steam powered generators that produced electricity. The electrical current ran through cables to a nearby station. From there it traveled out to other stations.

The same electric power system is still used today. Each track system has an electrified contact rail. This rail supplies electricity to power the subway trains. Each train car is equipped with four contact shoes. As the train passes over the contact rail, the shoes touch the rail. Electricity travels from the rail to the train cars.

Powerful generators created the electricity to run trains and equipment.

Electricity from the power plant also operates the stations' lights and fans.

After four years of construction, the first nine miles (14.5 km) of the New York City subway were ready for passengers. The line opened for service on October 27, 1904. Mayor George McClellan drove the first train. The mayor drove from City Hall to 103rd Street. At 7:00 that evening, the subway officially opened. Thousands of people paid five cents to take a ride on the historic new subway.

# STRAIGHT TO THE
# SOURCE

Writer Arthur Ruhl described a cave-in event that happened during subway tunnel construction:

*The tunnel here burrows under the existing subway . . . and its floor is about sixty feet [18 m] below the surface. . . . But the rock . . . lay in slanting strata, and one day, almost without warning, a huge section . . . simply slid diagonally from the easterly roof as a card slips out of a loosely shuffled pack. Every workman on the section was rushed to the spot in the hope that the damage could be repaired . . . but before the break could be properly shored, the areaways and front steps of the houses came tumbling down into the chasm. Parts of the front walls soon followed, and the crowd of idlers and nurse-maids and delivery boys who gathered . . . enjoyed the delectable experience of gazing into the very heart of each house . . . .*

Source: Arthur Ruhl. "Building New York's Subway." *Century Magazine*. NYCSubway.org, n.d. Web. Accessed February 13, 2017.

## Consider Your Audience

Adapt this passage for a different audience, such as your friends or family. Write a blog post describing the incident for the new audience. How does your post differ from the original text and why?

CHAPTER
# FOUR

# NEW YORK'S SUBWAY TODAY

After opening its first line on October 27, 1904, the New York City subway system continued to expand. In the early 1900s, the population of New York City lived mostly in Manhattan. Planners expanded the subway system to encourage people to move outside Manhattan. Most expansion occurred during the 40 years after the opening of the first route.

**Grand Central Station is a major hub for subways and other train systems in New York City.**

# SUBWAY MAINTENANCE

Maintaining New York City's subway lines is a challenging job. The subway has 666 miles (1,071 km) of track that need to be inspected on a regular basis. This enormous task is accomplished with people called track walkers and specialized track geometry cars. The cars detect and record problems as they travel along the subway tracks. Serious issues such as excessively worn or broken rails are dangerous. They can lead to train derailment.

## THE MOLE

More recent subway projects use a tunnel boring machine (TBM) to excavate a smooth, round tunnel. It is also known as a mole. TBMs can work in different types of ground, from soft and wet to hard or fractured rock. Modern TBMs have specialized discs and rotating cutters. They chew through even the hardest rock. Moles are lowered into the ground in separate pieces. Then they are assembled into building-sized machines. As the machine advances, rubble is hauled away on a conveyor. TBMs also act as a shield for tunnel workers.

One of the subway system's inspection and maintenance cars at a station

Track geometry cars use a combination of methods to take measurements as they pass over the rails. Video cameras record rail conditions. Ultrasonic testing, rotating lasers, and heat imaging systems collect data. Inside the car, trained workers analyze the information. They then order the necessary track repairs. The track geometry car's infrared sensors help detect electrical shorts, loose electrical connections, and worn cable insulation. If not repaired, these problems can cause fires.

Workers keep the system's trains clean and functioning properly.

Many parts of Manhattan are barely above sea level. This means water is a constant problem in the subway tunnels. Pumps must operate continuously

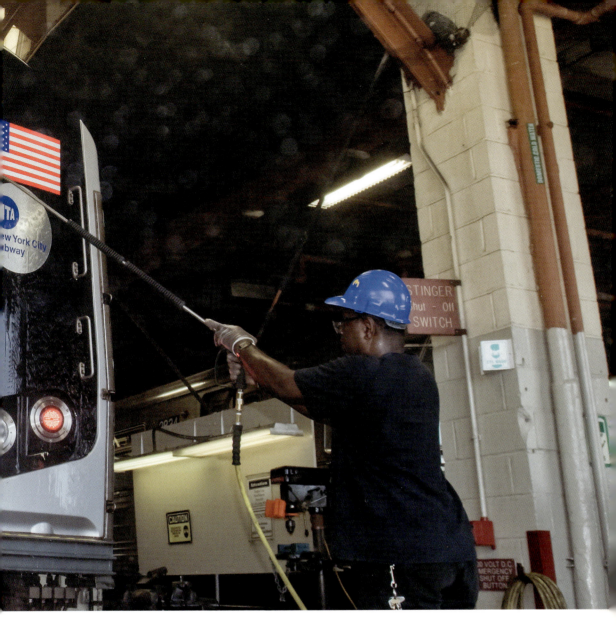

to keep water out of the underground system. The subway's electrical system and train cars also require ongoing maintenance.

## TRAIN CONTROL

Outdated machines are used all over the subway system. Subway officials warn that old equipment is dangerous. Several stations use machines installed in the 1930s to monitor trains. Old cloth-covered wires are a fire hazard. Updating technology on each route takes decades to complete. But New York transit officials are switching over to using a continuous two-way digital communication system. This radio signaling system uses equipment along the railroad as well as onboard sensors to determine the exact location and speed of trains. It increases train safety and train traffic. Trains can travel closer together without adjusting the braking distance needed to avoid collisions.

# SUBWAY UPGRADES

Advances in engineering, construction, and technology have changed the way the subway is constructed and run. But modernizing equipment is a slow and difficult process. It disrupts train service. Subways must be closed while work is being completed.

A subway redesign plan released in July 2016 features several technology upgrades. New subway cars will have digital signs, LED headlights, USB chargers, and Wi-Fi. Enhanced LED lighting and security cameras in cars and stations will improve commuter safety. Science and engineering is modernizing the way people travel in the New York City subway system.

## FURTHER EVIDENCE

Chapter Four discusses the maintenance and improvements being made to the New York City subway system. What are the main points made in this chapter? What evidence is included to support these points? Read the article at the website below. Does the information on the website support the points made by the chapter? What new information does it present?

### THE FUTURE OF THE NEW YORK CITY SUBWAY
abdocorelibrary.com/engineering-the-nyc-subway-system

# FAST FACTS

- The New York City subway system runs all day, every day, all year long.

- Engineer William Barclay Parsons designed the New York City subway system and oversaw its construction.

- Parsons designed a four-track system that is the most extensive in the world.

- Each track has an electrified third rail. Electricity passes to the train through a special piece called a shoe.

- Construction of the New York City subway system began in 1900. The first line opened on October 27, 1904.

- During cut-and-cover construction, workers dug trenches for the tunnels and covered the openings above with beams.

- A steel shield, drills, and dynamite were different methods used to tunnel through rock, sand, or wet soil.

- Workers called sandhogs worked in dangerous conditions underground to build the New York City subway system.

- New technologies in the New York City subway system include new digital signs, more LED lights, USB chargers, Wi-Fi, closed-circuit TV, and advanced security cameras onboard trains and alongside train tracks.

# STOP AND THINK

### Surprise Me

Chapter Two discusses the plans for building the New York City subway system. After reading this book, what two or three facts about building the subway did you find most surprising? Write a few sentences about each fact. Why did you find each fact surprising?

### Dig Deeper

After reading this book, what questions do you still have about the construction of the New York City subway system? With an adult's help, find a few reliable sources that can help you answer your questions. Write a paragraph about what you learned.

### Another View

This book talks about the design and building of the New York City subway system. As you know, every source is different. Ask a librarian or another adult to help you find another source about this project. Write a short essay comparing and contrasting the new source's point of view

with that of this book's author. What is the point of view of each author? How are they similar, and why? How are they different, and why?

## You Are There

This book discusses workers known as sandhogs doing their jobs in dangerous conditions underground. Imagine you are helping to build a subway tunnel. Write a letter home telling your friends about your experience. What is it like in the tunnel? What hardships and dangers do you deal with? Be sure to add plenty of detail to your notes.

# GLOSSARY

**chasm**
a deep hole in the ground

**colossal**
extremely large

**dredge**
to scoop out the bottom of a river bed

**excavation**
digging to make a hole

**geology**
the study of rocks and soil

**insatiable**
unable to be satisfied

**pneumatic**
operated by air pressure

**stationary**
not moving

**viaduct**
a long, high bridge or roadway

# LEARN MORE

## Books

Gagne, Tammy. *Women in Engineering*. Minneapolis, MN: Abdo Publishing, 2017.

Latham, Donna. *Bridges and Tunnels: Investigate Feats of Engineering with 25 Projects*. White River Junction, VT: Nomad Press, 2012.

Sandler, Martin W. *Secret Subway*. Washington, DC: National Geographic, 2009.

## Websites

To learn more about Building by Design, visit **abdobooklinks.com**. These links are routinely monitored and updated to provide the most current information available.

Visit **abdocorelibrary.com** for free additional tools for teachers and students.

# INDEX

## About the Author

Cecilia Pinto McCarthy has written several science and nature books for children. She also teaches environmental science programs at a nature sanctuary. She lives with her family north of Boston, Massachusetts.